Muslim Guide to Pandemics

By

Shaykh Muftī Saiful Islām

JKN Publications

First Published in October 2020

ISBN 978-1-909114-65-4

British Library Cataloguing in Publication Data
A catalogue record for this book is available from the British Library.

Publisher's Note:

Every care and attention has been put into the production of this book. If however, you find any errors they are our own, for which we seek Allāh's ﷻ forgiveness and the reader's pardon.

Published by:

JKN Publications
118 Manningham Lane
Bradford
West Yorkshire
BD8 7JF
United Kingdom

t: +44 (0) 1274 308 456 | w: www.jkn.org.uk | e: info@jkn.org.uk

Book Title: Muslim Guide to Pandemics

Author: Shaykh Muftī Saiful Islām

Printed by Mega Printing in Turkey

بسم الله الرحمن الرحيم

"In the Name of Allāh, the Most Beneficent, the Most Merciful"

Contents

BOOK TWO - *Shaykh Muftī Saiful Islām*

Muslim Guide to Pandemics

Introduction

All praises are due to Allāh ﷻ and may His peace and salutations be upon our noble Messenger ﷺ, upon the noble Companions ؓ and upon all those who follow their lifestyles.

Alhamdulillāh, it is a great privilege to have been able to complete this transcription. This kitāb is filled with reminders and advice from our honourable Shaykh, Muftī Saiful Islām Sāhib (hafizahullāh). The kitāb comprises of the many trials and tribulations we are to face. Our honourable Ustādh wonderfully provides advice from the hadīth and himself on ways to safeguard ourselves. We hope this book greatly benefits our readers and us all.

We request du'ās for Muftī Sāhib (hafizahullāh) and the publication team.

Bint Akkās
Graduate of Bahr Academy (Newcastle)
Shawwāl 1441 AH / May 2020

بِسۡمِ اللّٰهِ الرَّحۡمٰنِ الرَّحِیۡمِ

"In the name of Allāh ﷻ, the Most Beneficent, the Most Merciful"

Innumerable Blessings

My beloved readers, Allāh ﷻ has given us many favours. He has given us abundant blessings; in fact, Allāh ﷻ has given us everything that we have asked for! In the holy Qur'ān Allāh ﷻ mentions, **"And He grants you whatever you ask of Him."** Subhān-Allāh, the blessings are so numerous that we are unable to even count what Allāh ﷻ has bestowed on us:

وَإِنْ تَعُدُّوا نِعْمَةَ اللّٰهِ لَا تُحْصُوهَا ۗ إِنَّ اللّٰهَ لَغَفُورٌ رَّحِيمٌ ۞

"And if you want to count the blessings of Allāh you will not be able to. Indeed Allāh is the Most Forgiving, the Most Merciful." (16:18)

If we look at this Qur'anic verse, we will notice that the word ni'mat, in Arabic is wāhid i.e. singular. So Allāh ﷻ is saying that within that one ni'mat (blessing) there are other numerous ni'mats (blessings). If we are unable to count even one of them, just imagine the numerous and unlimited blessings, favours and bounties which He has bestowed upon us! Brothers and sisters, let us ask ourselves, how many times have we thanked Allāh ﷻ for all the innumerable blessings in our lives?

The first thing we must understand is that we have to be grateful to Allāh ﷻ . Gratitude is a very important quality that we should all possess. Allāh ﷻ says,

﴿ لَئِن شَكَرْتُمْ لَأَزِيدَنَّكُمْ ﴾

"If you are grateful, I will surely increase you (in favour)." (14:7)

May Allāh ﷻ grant us all the ability to show gratitude and thanks to Him. Āmīn.

How Many Years did you Live?

Many of us do not realise that our life in this world is indeed short. One of the questions we will be asked on the Day of Qiyāmah is:

﴿ كَمْ لَبِثْتُمْ فِي الْأَرْضِ عَدَدَ سِنِينَ ﴾

"How long did you stay in the earth, in terms of years?" (23:112)

Regardless of how long a person lived on earth, every single person will be asked this one question. From the first man till the last man, we will all be there, where Allāh ﷻ Himself will be asking this seemingly simple question. So, how will we respond?

On the Day of Judgement, people will be trembling, drowned in their own sweat. Subhān-Allāh! The scenario will be so catastrophic that people will be completely lost in their own worries. Even the prophets عليهم السلام will be saying, "Yā Rabbī sallim (O Allāh سبحانه وتعالى give us safety)!" They will want themselves to be saved and will not be worrying about anybody else.

يَوْمَ يَفِرُّ الْمَرْءُ مِنْ أَخِيهِ ﴿٣٤﴾ وَأُمِّهِ وَأَبِيهِ ﴿٣٥﴾ وَصَاحِبَتِهِ وَبَنِيهِ ﴿٣٦﴾ لِكُلِّ امْرِئٍ
مِّنْهُمْ يَوْمَئِذٍ شَأْنٌ يُغْنِيهِ ﴿٣٧﴾

"On that day a person will be running away from his own brother, from his own mother, from his own father, from his wife and his children; for every person amongst them on that day is a matter which will suffice him." **(80: 34-37)**

So, on the Day of Judgement, when that question will be put forward, the people will be in complete disbelief that they lived for years. Some will claim they lived for only 10 days, others will claim only one day. This will be to such an extent that one group will claim that they only stayed for a moment of time referred to as 'as-sā'ah' which nowadays we translate as one hour.

This is our life that we are chasing after day and night.

Purpose of Life

﴿وَمَا خَلَقْتُ الْجِنَّ وَالْإِنسَ إِلَّا لِيَعْبُدُونِ﴾

"And I have not created jinn and mankind except to worship Me." (51:56)

It is unfortunate to say that we seem to have completely forgotten the purpose which Allāh سبحانه وتعالى has created us for. Instead, we are running around, aimlessly, like headless chickens, for that sustenance which Allāh سبحانه وتعالى has already stipulated for us. We seem to aim with full concentration at these things. On the other hand, we do not seem to have time for salāh. We do not have time for coming to the madrasah or masjid on time. We cannot seem to make time for the holy Qur'ān!

Allāh سبحانه وتعالى Himself mentions:

﴿وَمَا مِن دَابَّةٍ فِي الْأَرْضِ إِلَّا عَلَى اللَّهِ رِزْقُهَا﴾

"And there is no creature on earth except that upon Allāh is its provision." (11:6)

Subhān-Allāh. Allāh سبحانه وتعالى mentions in Sūrah Mulk:

﴿هُوَ الَّذِي جَعَلَ لَكُمُ الْأَرْضَ ذَلُولًا فَامْشُوا فِي مَنَاكِبِهَا وَكُلُوا مِن رِّزْقِهِ وَإِلَيْهِ النُّشُورُ﴾

"It is He Who made the earth tame for you, so walk among its slopes and eat of His provision; to Him is the resurrection." (67:15)

So, Allāh ﷻ is telling us that He has made the earth easy for us!

فَامْشُوا فِي مَنَاكِبِهَا وَكُلُوا مِن رِّزْقِهِ ۞

"So walk on the corners of the earth and have your sustenance." (67:15)

The word فَامْشُوا has been used which means 'so walk.' Therefore, my beloved readers, we do not need to run around for sustenance! Just walk and we will attain whatever has been decreed.

I once met a brother and subhān-Allāh what he said was astonishing. He said, "I have 5 children and until I get 5 free hold houses, I am not going to stop earning. I work 18 hours and live on just one can of coke and one sandwich a day!"

Tell me my dear readers, is this the objective of a Muslim?

Even though Allāh ﷻ is telling us to walk for these things, we constantly chase after them day and night. Yet, the objective towards which He tells us to run, we fail to do so.

Let us take the example of the Jumu'ah Salāh. Allāh ﷻ says:

يَٰٓأَيُّهَا ٱلَّذِينَ ءَامَنُوٓا۟ إِذَا نُودِىَ لِلصَّلَوٰةِ مِن يَوْمِ ٱلْجُمُعَةِ فَٱسْعَوْا۟ إِلَىٰ ذِكْرِ ٱللَّهِ وَذَرُوا۟ ٱلْبَيْعَ ۚ ذَٰلِكُمْ خَيْرٌ لَّكُمْ إِن كُنتُمْ تَعْلَمُونَ ۝

"O you who believe! When the call is proclaimed for the salāh on the day of Friday, hasten to the remembrance of Allāh and leave off business, that is better for you if you know!" (62:9)

If we take a closer look at this Qur'anic verse we will notice that Allāh ﷻ has used the word فَٱسْعَوْا۟, meaning to hasten. So not just walk, but hasten quickly, and to what extent? To the extent that you leave your worldly transactions, subhān-Allāh.

How Were the Sahābah ﷺ when they Heard the Adhān?

Allāhu Akbar. Do you want to know what Allāh ﷻ says regarding the noble Sahābah ﷺ? He says رِجَالٌ (men). Some of us might question here that they were men but are we too not men? However, there is a big difference between them and us. Allāh ﷻ continues:

رِجَالٌ لَّا تُلْهِيهِمْ تِجَٰرَةٌ وَلَا بَيْعٌ عَن ذِكْرِ ٱللَّهِ وَإِقَامِ ٱلصَّلَوٰةِ وَإِيتَآءِ ٱلزَّكَوٰةِ ۙ يَخَافُونَ يَوْمًا تَتَقَلَّبُ فِيهِ ٱلْقُلُوبُ وَٱلْأَبْصَٰرُ ۝

"(True) men whom business and trade did not distract them nor makes them heedless from the remembrance of Allāh and

establishing salāh and giving zakāh, fearing a day in which hearts and visions will flip." (24:37)

This verse was revealed regarding the noble Sahābah رضي الله عنهم. As soon as they heard the ādhān, they would immediately stop their transactions.

Take the example of a blacksmith amongst them. He would be hitting the iron with his hammer but as soon as the ādhān echoed into his ears, he did not hit the iron once more. Rather, he threw the hammer behind his back and made his way to the masjid!

These were true men. Let us now ask ourselves, where are we aiming towards? Let us ponder over this and make the intention to correct our priorities.

May Allāh سبحانه وتعالى grant us all the ability to correct our priorities and please Him. Āmīn.

When it comes to Paradise, Allāh سبحانه وتعالى says:

وَسَارِعُوٓا إِلَىٰ مَغْفِرَةٍ مِّن رَّبِّكُمْ وَجَنَّةٍ عَرْضُهَا ٱلسَّمَٰوَٰتُ وَٱلْأَرْضُ أُعِدَّتْ لِلْمُتَّقِينَ ۞

"Race towards forgiveness from your Lord and a garden whose width is that (of the whole) of the heavens and the earth, prepared for the righteous." (3:133)

Those who understand the Arabic language will admire this verse. Allāh ﷻ has not merely told us to run, rather He has urged us to race one another. Hence, if somebody else is going quicker than you, then you should compete with him as you would in a race. For example, if an individual is reciting one juz of the holy Qur'ān everyday, then you should try to read two juz. If a friend is performing their five times salāh, you should aim to extend on that by performing your Awwābīn, Chāsht, Ishrāq and Tahajjud in'shā'Allāh. This is what we call competition and this is what the noble Sahābah did! It has been mentioned in the holy Qur'ān:

﴿ وَفِي ذَٰلِكَ فَلْيَتَنَافَسِ الْمُتَنَافِسُونَ ﴾

"For this let the competitors compete." (83:26)

Subhān-Allāh. Allāh ﷻ then says , if you want to meet Him,

﴿ فَفِرُّوا إِلَى اللَّهِ ﴾

"Then run to Allāh!" (51:50)

The ultimate goal and objective is Allāh ﷻ. So, here in this verse, there is no mention of competition. Rather, we are commanded to merely flee. There will be no need to look here and there, right and left when it comes to meeting Allāh ﷻ .We should just keep going!

This reminds me of an incident which occurred in 1997. Some of my readers might remember that in 1997 there was a blaze in Minā during hajj time. I was present there with my family including my father-in-law. When the tents began to burn and we could see the fire coming towards us, I said to my colleagues, "We need to move out!"

Some brothers objected, saying, "No, no! Just remain seated!" I rejected their response by saying, "You see the fire coming!" Still, there were other brothers saying, "Tawakkal a'lallāh (trust in Allāh)!" I informed them that such type of tawakkul was not required of us at that time and cried, "Brothers and sisters, let's get out from here!"

I can remember that at the time, there were some people on wheelchairs, yet, subhān-Allāh they were out and on top of the mountains before us. At this very moment فَفِرُّوْا إِلَى اللهِ came to mind.

While we were coming out, we met our respected teachers, Maulānā Bilāl Sāhib and Maulānā Abdur Rahīm Sāhib (may Allāh ﷻ protect them). I asked, "Hadhrat, where are you going?" and subhān-Allāh he simply replied, "فَفِرُّوْا إِلَى اللهِ!"

This was the thought on everyone's minds and "Run, run," were the words on everyone's tongues. I then thought to myself, "Subhān-Allāh, if this is the case in this world, what will be the case on the Day of Judgement? If this is the situation here, whereby even those who were on wheelchairs and physically disabled had left their

wheelchairs and ran to save their lives, what is going to be our situation on the Day of Judgement?!"
May Allāh ﷻ protect us all from all the punishments of Judgement Day. Āmīn!

Trials and Tribulations

Trials and tribulations will always happen, especially in this present day and age. The holy Prophet ﷺ said:

يَأْتِي عَلَى النَّاسِ زَمَانٌ الصَّابِرُ فِيهِمْ عَلَى دِينِهِ كَالْقَابِضِ عَلَى الْجَمْرِ

"A time will come upon people where a person persevering upon his dīn amongst them will be like one holding hot cinder (charcoal) in his hands."

It is apparent that we are going through this very time now and many more challenges are sure to come. An example of this can be seen in the hadīth:

لَيَأْتِيَنَّ عَلَى النَّاسِ زَمَانٌ لَّا يَبْقَى أَحَدٌ إِلَّا أَكِلَ الرِّبَا فَإِنْ لَّمْ يَأْكُلْهُ أَصَابَهُ مِنْ بُخَارِهِ

"A time will certainly come upon the people in which no one will remain except those who consume interest and even if he does not consume it then its vapour will reach him."

What is meant here by, *'its vapour will reach him?'* We can answer this question by way of common example. If you are not directly involved in interest, you will be indirectly eating from it. How? You will be eating from the house of a person who is consuming interest! The Prophet ﷺ says,

وَالَّذِي نَفْسِي بِيَدِهِ لَا تَذْهَبُ الدُّنْيَا حَتَّى يَمُرَّ الرَّجُلُ عَلَى الْقَبْرِ فَيَتَمَرَّغُ عَلَيْهِ وَيَقُولُ يَا لَيْتَنِي كُنْتُ مَكَانَ صَاحِبِ هٰذَا الْقَبْرِ وَلَيْسَ بِهِ الدِّيْنُ إِلَّا الْبَلَاءُ

"By Him, in Whose Hand my life is, the world will not come to an end until a person will be passing by a grave and he will be tossing on it and he will say, 'I wish I was the occupant of this grave,' not because of religion but because of calamity."

These people will not be expressing this wish because they are inclined to meet Allāh ﷻ due to the strength of their dīn. Rather, it will be because of the trials and tribulations which he is met with and due to the depression and hardships that he is facing.

Some Shocking Scenarios

One of my adult students informed me of the following incident:

She was once in the park in which there was a pond. While she was walking, her eyes suddenly fell onto a youngster, jumping into the pond. My student thought to herself, "Why is this girl doing this?"

So, my student went and grabbed the youngster and asked her what she was doing. The youngster replied "I want to kill myself!" When she was asked regarding her age and why she wanted to kill herself, the girl replied, "l failed my GCSE's and I do not know how to face my family. So, I thought to myself that it is better I commit suicide than face my parents."

Subhān-Allāh! Just because of failing her GCSE exams, this is what this individual had come to! A 16 year old was so depressed about how she is going to meet her family members.

There was another incident of a sister considering suicide one night when it was around 2 or 3am. I happened to look at my mobile and my eyes fell on the message from the sister which read,

'Muftī Sāhib, I am leaving this world. I am committing suicide. Please perform my janāzah and take my children to your madrasah.'

I thought to myself, "What am I going to do at this time? This woman is going to commit suicide!" One of my graduate students who knew this lady came to mind. I immediately called her and told her to go and save this woman.

Respected readers, these effects of depression are just a small fraction of the problems we are to face. Allāh ﷻ has already informed us in the holy Qur'ān:

وَلَنَبْلُوَنَّكُمْ بِشَيْءٍ مِّنَ الْخَوْفِ وَالْجُوعِ وَنَقْصٍ مِّنَ الْأَمْوَالِ وَالْأَنفُسِ وَالثَّمَرَاتِ ۗ وَبَشِّرِ الصَّابِرِينَ ۞

"And We will surely test you with something of fear and hunger and a loss of wealth and lives and fruits, but give glad tidings to the patient." (2:155)

Those who are familiar with the Arabic language, will understand that in this verse, Allāh ﷻ has told us what will come in the exam. If a student is aware of what questions will appear on the paper, then he will come to the exam room prepared for the exam.

Now the question, 'Will the test be big?' may arise. If we take a closer look at the verse, we notice that Allāh ﷻ has used the word شَيْءٌ which is nakirah (indefinite), implying a small amount.

What is the Prize for Succeeding?

Allāh ﷻ ends the verse with:

وَبَشِّرِ الصَّابِرِينَ ۞

"And give glad tidings to the patient." (2:155)

For all these problems which we are to face, Allāh ﷻ is saying that we merely need to be patient in order for us to receive the glad tidings. How can this be so simple? Imagine saying, "Glad tidings to you," to a man who has recently lost his father. It is likely that he will become very angry and shout, "Why on earth are you giving me glad tidings upon the loss of my father?!"

Beloved readers, we need to understand that as a result of a person's patience and perseverance, he will gain immense rewards. These are the glad tidings referred to in the verse mentioned above.

Patience

﴿ الَّذِينَ إِذَا أَصَابَتْهُم مُّصِيبَةٌ قَالُوا إِنَّا لِلَّهِ وَإِنَّا إِلَيْهِ رَاجِعُونَ ﴾

"Those who, when a calamity afflicts them, they say, 'Indeed, we belong to Allāh and indeed to Him we are returning.'" (2:156)

Allāh ﷻ uses the word إِذَا in order to imply that whenever a difficulty befalls us, we should deal with it at that exact time, in other words, immediately. So respected readers, let us adopt this quality of patience right at the beginning of any calamity, in-shā-Allāh.

To highlight this quality even further let us take a look at the hadīth of our beloved Prophet ﷺ wherein he has mentioned:

إِنَّمَا الصَّبْرُ عِنْدَ الصَّدْمَةِ الأُوْلَى

"Verily, patience is at the first stroke of a calamity."

Below is the incident which is the background of the very hadīth. Sayyidunā Anas ibn Mālik ؓ narrates:

The Prophet ﷺ passed by a woman who was weeping beside a grave. He told her to fear Allāh ﷻ and be patient. She said to him , "Go away, for you have not been afflicted with a calamity like mine." And she did not recognize him. Then, she was informed that he was the Prophet ﷺ. So she went to the house of the Prophet ﷺ and there she did not find any guard. Then she said to him, "I did not recognize you." He responded, "Verily, patience is at the first stroke of a calamity."

Mere Memories?

In todays world, a lot of things become affected by customs and traditions. For instance, when somebody passes away, families and friends recite the holy Qur'ān and perform extra dhikr for a fixed number of days. After those days are finished, their i'bādat and sending rewards to the deceased also come to an end. Why is it that when parents pass away, only those obedient children actually remember them and even then this occurs at the minimal of once a year, on the death anniversary? Why is it that even parents become a distant memory when in reality, we should remember them all the time?

Respected readers, let us take our honourable scholar, Muftī Taqi Uthmāni Sāhib (hafizahullāh) as an example to follow. He says, "My father called me one day and said to me, 'Son, we will all have to leave. I will have to leave and I want you to remember me. People forget those who have passed away.' Then he uttered these unusual and strange words:

لیکن اتنا جلدی مجھے مت بھولنا

"But don't forget me so quickly."

Muftī Taqi Uthmāni Sāhib (hafizahullāh) says, "These words stuck to my mind and even now, after 40 years, these words have not left my mind. I remember him everyday and that is the way we ought to remember our parents."

My Father's Demise

As a child, I never managed to fully understand the respect of a father. I began my madrasah studies at Dārul-Ulūm Bury at the age of 14 and therefore, I did not even have the chance to fully get to know and understand my father. After returning to my family, a week after the graduation, my father had passed away.

After reciting the holy Qur'ān for my father, I saw him in a dream. I will forever remember this one statement which he made to me in my dream, "Son, you do not need to grieve because I always receive whatever you send me."

Many of us do not realise the great rewards of certain a'māl (deeds) we do. Whether it be helping the madrasah or masjid, or promoting the work of dīn, the rewards are immense. My father himself, left behind a great example that others have benefitted from. One particular uncle came to me after a janāzah and told me that he will send his son to the madrasah. The man had seen my father in a good state in a dream. This man wished to act in the same way as my beloved father.

A very close friend of my father once came to me and narrated a dream he had, wherein my father was calling him. In the dream, my father was showing him three big buildings and pointed out that one of those buildings was waiting for him. My father then asked the man to come quickly and meet him. This close friend of my father was unable to believe it. I told him, "In-shā-Allāh you will achieve Jannah. You are lucky that he is waiting for you and has already reserved a building for you!"

We Return to Allāh ﷻ

ٱلَّذِينَ إِذَآ أَصَٰبَتۡهُم مُّصِيبَةٞ قَالُوٓاْ إِنَّا لِلَّهِ وَإِنَّآ إِلَيۡهِ رَٰجِعُونَ ۝

"Those who when disaster strikes them, they say, 'Indeed we belong to Allāh and to Him we shall return.'" (2:156)

Nowadays, we seem to perceive that 'innā lillāh' is only recited at the news of someone's death. The reality is that whenever we are faced with any calamity, be it big or small, we should say 'innā lillāhi wa innā ilaihi rāji'ūn.'

In the hadīth we are clearly informed of four of the specific occasions in which we should recite this:

1. When pricked by a thorn
2. When the shoelace snaps
3. When a mosquito bites
4. When the lights go off

However, in our present day and age, when the lights go off, we have the habit of swearing and showing anger! We fail to recite this phrase 'innā lillāhi wa innā ilaihi rāji'ūn' at the very beginning of the calamity.

May Allāh ﷻ grant us all the ability to utter this phrase when faced with any calamity. Āmīn!

Allāh ﷻ is Khāliq (Creator) and we are Makhlūq (Creation)

The creation have no right to contradict, object or complain about any decree of Allāh ﷻ. Allāh ﷻ has the full authority to take a person back to Himself whenever He wishes. Why? Because we are His creation.

The Journey

We are all on a journey. Our journey commenced from ālam-e-arwāh (world of souls). There are four ā'lams (worlds):

1. **Ā'lam-e-Arwāh (Realm of the souls before birth)** - This is the world of souls where everyone waits to come to the dunyā.

2. **Ā'lam-e-Dunyā (Realm of the worldly life)** - This is the place of practice where each of us are temporarily residing.
3. **Ā'lam-e-Barzakh (Life of the grave after death)** - This stage of our journey will be a place of sleep for those who had achieved their purpose in life of worshipping Allāh ﷻ
4. **Ālame-e-Ākhirah (Life of the Hereafter)** - This is where the retribution or reward for people's actions of the world will take place.

A Dream Regarding the Life of Barzakh

I once saw a dream regarding my father-in-law, Muftī Tālib Uddīn Sāhib رحمه الله. He was a great scholar of Islām who used to live in Oldham. In this dream there were also many other scholars. When my father-in-law met me, I asked him, "O my father-in-law, will you tell me how you faired in front of Allāh ﷻ?" Subhān-Allāh, what a beautiful answer he responded with, "O my son-in-law, now is just the time to sleep." Immediately, the following hadīth came to my mind:

نَمْ كَنَوْمَةِ الْعَرُوْسِ

"Sleep like the night of the bride (wedding)."

I said to him, "O my father-in-law, you deserve it. All my life, from the moment I have got to know you, I have seen you toiling and working very hard. You stayed awake all night in tahajjud, in dhikr, in propogating the dīn and in teaching. Now you deserve it; now you need to sleep. It is people like you who can be doing this. Allāh ﷻ has bestowed you with this favour."

May Allāh ﷻ grant us all peace in the Hereafter. Āmīn.

No Return Back

Some people only realize the mistakes of their life at the time of death . They then ask to be returned to the world so that they can carry out good deeds.

حَتَّىٰٓ إِذَا جَآءَ أَحَدَهُمُ ٱلْمَوْتُ قَالَ رَبِّ ٱرْجِعُونِ ﴿٩٩﴾ لَعَلِّىٓ أَعْمَلُ صَٰلِحًا فِيمَا تَرَكْتُ ﴿١٠٠﴾

"Until, when death comes to one of them he says. 'My Lord, send me back.' That I might do righteousness in that which I left behind." (23: 99-100)

Allāh's ﷻ response to these statements is displayed in the very same verse,

كَلَّا ۚ إِنَّهَا كَلِمَةٌ هُوَ قَائِلُهَا ۖ وَمِن وَرَائِهِم بَرْزَخٌ إِلَىٰ يَوْمِ يُبْعَثُونَ ۞

"Never! These are words he is saying and behind them is Barzakh until the day they will be resurrected." (23:100)

So before any regret enters our minds, we need to work in the best way we can, to please Allāh ﷻ.

May Allāh ﷻ make us all from His obedient servants. Āmīn.

Signs of the Last Day

The Messenger of Allāh ﷺ said:

يُوشِكُ أَنْ يَأتِيَ عَلَى النَّاسِ زَمَانٌ لَا يَبْقَى مِنَ الْإِسْلَامِ إِلَّا اسْمُهُ

"A time will come upon the people when nothing of Islām will remain except its name."

These signs have already come to us. There are Muslims we see in many places who have the Islāmic names but they do not know the kalimah properly. They are not aware of what zakāh or salāh is. They do not even know what the month of Ramadhān is. The only thing that remains is their statement, "We are Muslims."

Our Experience in Turkey

A few years ago, myself and my wife travelled to Turkey. A sister noticed my wife adopting the full hijāb. The sister came to us and she asked my wife if she could wear the hijāb and the niqāb my wife was wearing. The sister could remember that her grandmother used to wear the same type of attire and she desired to experience how they used to dress. I asked her if she was Muslim. Subhān-Allāh, she replied that she was because her parents and grandparents were Muslims. Thus, only the name will remain.

In the full text of the previous hadīth, mention has also been made that only the written form of the holy Qur'ān will remain.

لَا يَبْقٰى مِنَ الْقُرْاٰنِ إِلَّا رَسْمُهٗ

"There will not remain from the Qur'an except its written form."

In other words, the holy Qur'ān will be displayed on our shelves but we will not be reading them. This is a very likely consequence of none other than the SOCIAL MEDIA!

The Attack of Social Media

In short, social media has completely ruined many of us! Once, during a discussion with some friends, they admitted that there was a time when they would recite the holy Qur'ān in abundance but now, they have stopped reciting. When questioned why, they replied, "We are so busy with our social media and as a result, nobody reads the holy Qur'ān."

Those who have become hāfiz of the holy Qur'ān are not concentrating on the holy Qur'ān and nor do they exert much effort into it. Why is this the case? This is due to them being apparently busy. With what? With social media. This results in them forgetting the holy Qur'ān!

Advice to Huffāz Students

Some recommendations for the huffāz students not to fall into this trap are as follows:

1. Recite at least one juz' of the holy Qur'ān daily. In this way we will manage to complete roughly 12 khatms (completion) in the year.
2. Try to keep track by following the Islamic Calender so we can also be aware of the Islāmic dates. In this way, one khatm will be recited every Islamic month.

Answer to Parents

A parent once came to me and expressed a concern that their child will not be able to complete both school and madrasah together. After replying that the child would be able to, I asked the parent to call the child. The following conversation took place:

Myself (to the child): Have you got a mobile phone?

Child: Yes, an iPhone 8.

Myself: If you have got an iPhone 8, then that is the first mistake you have made. How many hours do you spend on it?

Child: About 5 to 6 hours a day.

Myself (to the parents): Father, mother, have you received your answer? Why is the child unable to fulfil both school and madrasah? Possibly because he will be spending that time on his phone, on social media. Take away his mobile phone and he will be able to complete both together. Thereby, he will accomplish success in both fields in-shā-Allāh.

By providing our children with mobile phones, ipods, ipads, tablets and other gadgets, we have destroyed them. Below is an example of what we call addiction:

I was invited to a house for a da'wat (meal). The father of three informed his children, "Muftī -Sāhib is coming so you must shake hands with him and serve the food."

While I was there, I was looking at them for about an hour but not one of them would look up. Why? Because they were so engrossed and occupied on their laptops and ipods. At times, thinking that I was not looking, the father tried to pull the devices away from them. The children began squealing, "No, I'm going to lose!"

Furthermore, at the time of my entry and departure from the house the father instructed his children to make salām. The three children merely looked up and then straight back down without any salām.

This is what we call addiction and we only have ourselves to blame for providing our children with these devices in the first place.

May Allāh ﷻ protect us all and our children from the trials and temptations of these devices. Āmīn.

Occupied yet Devoid

Another sign of Qiyāmāh is:

مَسَاجِدُهُمْ عَامِرَةٌ

"Their masājid will be occupied but devoid of guidance."

There are many masājid that will appear externally beautiful however, internally they will be devoid of guidance.

A brother once asked me, "Muftī Sāhib! What kind of masjid is yours? Our masjid is so big. We have re-built it and placed this chandelier worth £60,000! Look at your masjid - it has no chandelier; there is nothing there!"

This brother was competing and that itself is a sign of Qiyāmah.

Fitnah in Oneself

In 'Hujjatullāhil Bālighah,' Shāh Waliullāh Muhaddith Dehlawi ﷬ provides some detailed explanations of the different categories of fitnah.

إِعْلَمْ أَنَّ الْفِتَنَ عَلي أَقْسَامٍ

"Know that there are different types of fitnah."

He mentions that a person will find so much fitnah within himself., to the extent that his heart becomes very hardened.

فَلَا يَجِدُ حَلَاوَةَ الطَّاعَةِ وَلَا لَذَّةَ الْمُنَاجَاةِ

"Hence, he will not taste the sweetness of obedience nor of speaking to Allāh ﷻ."

Due to the consumption of our time with social media, this great deed of salāh and du'ā has somewhat become eradicated from our lives.

Allāh سُبْحَانَهُ وَتَعَالَىٰ mentions in the holy Qur'ān:

ثُمَّ قَسَتْ قُلُوبُكُم مِّنۢ بَعْدِ ذَٰلِكَ فَهِيَ كَالْحِجَارَةِ أَوْ أَشَدُّ قَسْوَةً ۚ وَإِنَّ مِنَ الْحِجَارَةِ لَمَا يَتَفَجَّرُ
مِنْهُ الْأَنْهَٰرُ ۚ وَإِنَّ مِنْهَا لَمَا يَشَّقَّقُ فَيَخْرُجُ مِنْهُ الْمَآءُ ۚ وَإِنَّ مِنْهَا لَمَا يَهْبِطُ مِنْ خَشْيَةِ اللَّهِ ۗ
وَمَا اللَّهُ بِغَٰفِلٍ عَمَّا تَعْمَلُونَ ۝

"Then your hearts became hardened after that, being like stones or even harder. For indeed, there are stones from which rivers burst forth, there are some of them that split open and water comes out and there are some of them that fall down for fear of Allāh. And Allāh is not unaware of what you do." (2:74)

Subhān-Allāh! Even stones have those qualities which we fail to adopt.

Coming to the Masjid

Shāh Waliullāh Muhaddith Dehlawi رَحِمَهُ ٱللَّٰهُ mentions that a person's heart will become hard to such an extent that he will dislike coming to the masjid.

Nowadays, many of our youngsters do not like coming to the masjid. We have observed on the day of Jumu'ah that the youth are the last to enter as well as the first to leave. Some do not even find the sermon and immediately exit the masjid after the fardh. So, they neglect the sunnah mu'akkadah!

The majority of the youth and even adults are unaware of the immense rewards mentioned regarding this in the ahādīth:

سَبْعَةٌ يُظِلُّهُمُ اللهُ فِي ظِلِّهِ يَوْمَ لَا ظِلَّ إِلَّا ظِلُّهُ

"Allāh will give shade to seven categories of people on the day when there shall be no shade but His."

Out of these seven, one of them is:

شَابٌّ نَشَأَ فِيْ عِبَادَةِ رَبِّهِ

"A youngster who was nourished in the worship of Allāh ﷻ."

Another type of person out of the seven is:

رَجُلٌ قَلْبُهُ مُعَلَّقٌ فِيْ الْمَسَاجِدِ

"A man whose heart is attached to the masjid." (Bukhārī, Muslim)

In other words, whenever this man leaves the masjid, he is always wanting to return to it. So, my brothers! When it comes to the masjid do not be like the bird in the cage. Once it goes out, it does not want to come back in. Rather, be like the fish which does not want to get out. When it does, it yearns to return back.

Black Dots

In the hadīth, the Prophet ﷺ mentions:

"When a person commits a sin, a black dot forms on his heart. If he continues to commit sins, these black dots continue to increase. If then he makes repentance, his heart is polished. However, if he continues with sin, his heart becomes completely rusted."

What happens next? Then, Allāh ﷻ seals the hearts, eyes and ears thereby, nothing good enters them. Deaf, dumb and blind, they will not return.

What is meant by deaf, dumb and blind? In this context, it refers to being spiritually deaf, dumb and blind.

Allāh ﷻ makes this clear in another verse in which He says:

﴿فَإِنَّهَا لَا تَعْمَى الْأَبْصَارُ وَلَٰكِن تَعْمَى الْقُلُوبُ الَّتِي فِي الصُّدُورِ﴾

"Verily, it is not the eyes that are blind but the hearts have become blind." (22:46)

So, they possess the eyesight but are devoid of insight.

Missing 3 Jumu'ah Prayers

In the hadīth, it has been mentioned that a person who continuously misses three Jumu'ah prayers, has his heart sealed by Allāh ﷻ. Thereafter no good enters. We see that our youngsters who attend college, university and work do not read their Jumu'ah prayer. Simultaneously, they are extremely anti-masjid and dislike coming to salāh. This is because Allāh ﷻ has sealed their hearts. Those hearts have now hardened.

"I Can't Cry!"

A Companion ؓ narrates, "The Prophet ﷺ was addressing us with an emotional speech. Everybody was crying, however I could not cry. I thought to myself, "Subhān-Allāh, everyone is crying but I can't cry!"

In our days, matters are different. When one person is crying, the majority question, "Why is he crying? What is wrong with him?!"

This is another example which makes apparent that the hearts have become hard.

The holy Prophet ﷺ said to the Companion ؓ, "*The lack of tears is due to hard heartedness and the hard heartedness is due to excessive sinning. Excessive sinning is because we have forgotten death. Forgetting death is due to high expectation. High expectations are because of the love of the world and the love of the world is the root of all evils!"*

Dīn Over Dunyā

The imminent result of the love of the dunyā will be, that we will leave the Ākhirah. In short, you cannot hold both the dunyā and Ākhirah in the same degree.

بَلْ تُؤْثِرُونَ ٱلْحَيَوٰةَ ٱلدُّنْيَا ﴿١٦﴾ وَٱلْـَٔاخِرَةُ خَيْرٌ وَأَبْقَىٰٓ ﴿١٧﴾

"But you prefer the worldly life while the Hereafter is better and ever-lasting." (87: 16-17)

Sayyidunā Alī ﷺ beautifully mentions that the dunyā and Ākhirah are like two co-wives. When one wife is happy, the other becomes angry. So, if we want to make the dunyā happy, the Ākhirah will be angry and vice versa. Sayyidunā Alī ﷺ continues saying, "So give priority to that which will remain over that which will finish." Just as the saying goes 'dīn over dunyā.'

Wasting Time

A sister sent me a letter in which she wrote:

"There was a time I used to recite many juz' of the holy Qur'ān. I used to do my tasbīhāt, ma'mūlāt, durūd sharīf and everything. Now I cannot even open the Qur'ān and read one ruku' because I am so addicted with social media. From one comedy to another and from one clip to another, I am wasting my time! What is the cure for this?"

This spiritual illness of wasting time has become a problem for every one of us, except for whom Allāh ﷻ wills.

Fitnah within the Family

Whilst sitting in my office, I am able to see these cases. The number of divorces we deal with on a Monday morning is immense. On a weekly basis we usually perform one or two marriages but unfortunately, we have to deal with 10 times more divorces!

Allāh ﷻ says:

وَمِنْ ءَايَٰتِهِۦٓ أَنْ خَلَقَ لَكُم مِّنْ أَنفُسِكُمْ أَزْوَٰجًا لِّتَسْكُنُوٓا۟ إِلَيْهَا ۞

"And from among His signs are that He has created you in pairs so that you can find peace." (30:21)

In this present era, many men experience the complete opposite of what is mentioned in the Qur'anic āyah. Instead of finding peace, the depression and difficulty of the man increases.

During work, a boss became angry with his employee and shouted, "Go to hell!" When the employee came home, his wife asked him why he was home. He replied, "My boss said go to hell, so I came home!" Unfortunately, this is the reality nowadays, where the man sees his home as hell. May Allāh ﷻ save us.

The Prophet ﷺ with Sayyidah Ā'ishah ﵂

The love and conduct of Nabī ﷺ with his wives was beautiful. Sayyidah Ā'ishah ﵂ says, "We used to sit down to eat and the Prophet ﷺ would place his lips on that exact part of the bone on which I chewed. I used to drink water and he would place his blessed lips on that part and drink from the same glass."

Sayyidunā Abdullāh ibn Rawāhah ﵁ was once sitting with his wife when he suddenly started to cry. When his wife began to shed tears too, he asked her, "Why are you crying?" She replied, "Because I saw you cry." The husband's crying was enough to stimulate the wife to cry as well! This was the kind of bond between spouses in the past. Nowadays, this connection has considerably diminished.

It has been mentioned in a hadīth that a time will come when destruction of a person will be in the hands of his wife and children. They will tease and taunt him of poverty. They will place those burdens on him which he cannot cope with; 'do or die' he has to listen. These are trials we see with our very own eyes.

اَلْفِتَنُ الَّتِيْ تَمُوْجُ كَمَوْجِ الْبَحْرِ
Fitnah like Tidal Waves

There will be those trials which like tidal waves will destroy the entire city. In reply to a bedouin, the holy Prophet ﷺ once said:

إِذَا وُسِّدَ الأَمْرُ إِلَى غَيْرِ أَهْلِه فَانْتَظِرِ السَّاعَةَ

"When matters will be given to those who do not deserve it, then wait for Qiyāmah."

People will be desiring various posts such as president, masjid leader and more. Even though they are not deserving of the post they will be granted it.

Scholars have mentioned that there are two meanings of the hadīth. One is that it is a sign of Qiyāmah. The second meaning is that it is the Qiyāmah of the particular organisation. This is due to the certain individual not having the expertise for the particular field.

The Way of the Great Leaders

When Sayyidunā Abū Bakr was in his last moments, he called Sayyidunā Uthmān Ghanī. Sayyidunā Abū Bakr ordered Sayyidunā Uthmān to write down the name of the person who will succeed him. At that time, Sayyidunā Abū Bakr fell into a coma. Whilst the great leader was unconscious, Sayyidunā Uthmān wrote down the name of Umar. Suddenly, Sayyidunā Abū Bakr regained consciousness and the following conversation took place:

Sayyidunā Abū Bakr: What did you write?
Sayyidunā Uthmān: I wrote.
Sayyidunā Abū Bakr: What?
Sayyidunā Uthmān: I wrote the name of Umar.

Sayyidunā Abū Bakr: You wrote the name of the person I intended to dictate. If you had written your name O Uthmān, you are well deserving of the post as well. However, I am very happy that I am leaving this world while there is no rivalry for leadership.

Another Great Incident

Sayyidunā Abdullāh ibn Abbās ﷺ once noticed Sayyidunā Umar ﷺ very worried and concerned. Below is the conversation which had taken place:

Sayyidunā Abdullāh ibn Abbās ﷺ: O Amīrul Muminīn, why are you so worried?
Sayyidunā Umar ﷺ: I am thinking about who will take this responsibility after me.
Sayyidunā Abdullāh ibn Abbās ﷺ: Do you not see these great, senior Companions of the Prophet ﷺ?
Sayyidunā Umar ﷺ: Do you know what it takes to be in this position?
He then uttered these golden words: A person who is able to take this khilāfat (leadership) on board is he who is:

1. Strong but not harsh
2. Soft but not weak
3. Generous but not extravagant
4. He withholds but is not miserly.

Subhān-Allāh, there is a fine line between each of the two pairs of qualities.

May Allāh ﷻ enable us all to adopt these golden qualities. Āmīn!

Natural Instincts

Another trial will be that people will lose their natural instincts. Something which is good will be seen as bad and something which is bad will be seen as good.

Allāh ﷻ states:

لَقَدْ خَلَقْنَا الْإِنسَانَ فِي أَحْسَنِ تَقْوِيمٍ ۞

"We have certainly created man in the best form." (95:4)

Despite this, in this present day and age, we as humans are doing those things which even animals would not do. In addition, those unnatural things are becoming legalised! In schools, children will be taught that these things are normal. They claim as normal that which the divine punishments had been sent down by our Creator!

May Allāh ﷻ protect us all. Āmīn!

Did you Know?

Did you know that many disasters are also trials? The earthquakes, tsunamis, plagues, famine and many other disasters are trials. We notice that before one disaster finishes, another one erupts.

May Allāh ﷻ save us all. Āmīn!

Trust will be Taken Away

In the hadīth it has been mentioned that one will be walking around to find someone who is honest and trustworthy but they will not be able to find them.

Sayyidunā Hudhaifah ؓ says, "In the beginning of Islām I could go to anybody and do transactions. If he was a Muslim, his faith would make sure that he completes the transaction properly with honesty. If he was not a Muslim, he would return the money back as the society was very clean and pristine."

Then he says, "In my later times, I only did transactions with certain people. A time will come when people will be looking for a person who is honest. He will be directed to a 'trustworthy' person in a far away land. After travelling so far to meet this person, he will return saying that the man does not have even an iota of trust! Yet, he will be classed as a very trustworthy person."

Digging Too Deep

There will be people who will delve into the depths of the holy Qur'ān. They will look into the intricacies and the ambiguous verses, then lead themselves and others to misguidance. In reality, when we do not know the meaning, we should simply say, "Allāh ﷻ knows best." Instead, there are a group of people who will dig so deep, to the extent that they will be misguided.

May Allāh ﷻ protect us all from this. Āmīn!

Disrespect

Another fitnah is when people will be swearing at our pious predecessors. Nowadays, we see people pointing fingers at Imām Abū Hanīfah ﵀ and the other Imāms.

I was part of an extremely active whatsapp group. One day, I was flicking through the messages when suddenly I came across a message which read, 'I blame Abū Hanīfah for all this mess.'

Innā lillāhi wa innā ilaihi rāji'ūn! I immediately went off the group. Respected readers, if this is the case, then we are becoming mujtahid ourselves. Without knowing ourselves how to recite the holy Qur'ān and salāh properly, we are pointing fingers and objecting to the great scholars.

It is extremely important to trust our pious predecessors and to think only good. First, bad thoughts enter the mind like, 'I think they hid something,' or, 'they did not tell us the truth.' After this, the people start to say ill things about them and the end result is that they become misguided!

Gobsmacked

A person once came to me and said, "This Ma'āriful Qur'ān by Muftī Muhammad Shafī Uthmāni Sāhib ﷺ is nonsense!" I was shocked! I replied to him, "You have read only one line and you are saying this!" This same individual also called me Mushrik.

May Allāh ﷻ forgive us all. Āmīn!

مِنْهَا فِتْنَةُ ظُهُوْرِ الْقَدَرِيَّةِ

Rejecting Taqdīr

There will be a group of people who completely reject taqdīr. They will believe that they are the creator of their own deeds and will ignore taqdīr.

Someone once asked Sayyidunā Alī رضي الله عنه to inform them about taqdīr. The great khalīfa رضي الله عنه replied, "This is a very dark road, do not try to go on it." The man asked again and Sayyidunā Alī رضي الله عنه replied, "It is a very deep ocean, do not attempt to dive into it." Yet again, the man asked. This time, the wise leader replied, "It is a secret of Allāh تعالى that has been hidden from you."

How do we Save Ourselves?

Sayyidunā Uqbah ibn Āmir رضي الله عنه once asked Rasūlullāh ﷺ, "How do we achieve salvation?" Our beloved Prophet Muhammad ﷺ mentioned 3 things:

1. أَمْسِكْ عَلَيْكَ لِسَانَكَ **(Control your tongue)**

If we manage to safeguard our tongues, we will be saved from many trials and tribulations.

A person once came to a scholar and said, "I heard about your friend." Thereafter, the following conversation took place:

Scholar: Before you tell me about my friend, I want to take you through this triple filter test.

Man: Ok.

Scholar: I want to take you through 3 things before you narrate to me about my friend. Firstly, is whatever you are going to tell me about my friend, true or not?

Man: I do not know; I heard it from another person.

Scholar: So brother, you want to say something to me and you do not know if it is true or false? That is the first filter. You heard it from a 3rd person. Ok, secondly, is it something good or bad about him?

Man: Brother, it is something bad.

Scholar: So you want to tell me something bad about him and you do not know if it is true or not. Ok, thirdly, never mind him, is it going to be beneficial to me or not?

Man: No. It is not going to be beneficial to you. It is going to hurt you because he is your friend.

Scholar: Brother! You want to tell me something about him which might not be true, is bad and it will not benefit me. Why are you telling me in the first place?

If we all try to adopt this triple filter test, it will surely prove beneficial. It will allow us to save a lot of time! Personally, it saves me a good 3 or 4 hours of time everyday.
In a hadīth it has been mentioned:

كَفٰى بِالْمَرْءِ كَذِبًا أَنْ يُّحَدِّثَ بِكُلِّ مَا سَمِعَ

"It is sufficient for a person to be a liar that he says everything he hears."

In this modern day and age, we must be very careful before sending messages around.

2. **وَلْيَسَعْكَ بَيْتُكَ** ***(Let your house be sufficient for you)***

Try not to go here and there too often with friends. Try to come out only for fulfilling the fardh obligations, any necessities and for seeking knowledge.

3. **وَابْكِ عَلٰى خَطِيْئَتِكَ** ***(And cry over your sins)***

If we act upon these 3 pieces of advice, we are sure to be protected from trials and tribulations in-shā-Allāh.

Some more Advice

1. Do not point your fingers at others. Always remember that when we point one finger at someone else, four fingers are pointing back at us.
2. Always have good thoughts about others.

3. Take that which is clear and leave what is dirty. In other words, look at the good qualities of people instead of the bad.

In conclusion, if we bring the Islamic teachings into our lives, we will see happiness. Our every day dealings as well as our social interactions within and outside the family will be positive and in-shā-Allāh, Allāh ﷻ will guide us all! We need to persevere and strive in the path of Allāh ﷻ.

May Allāh ﷻ give us all the tawfīq. Āmīn!

Taking Precautions

Introduction

All praises be to Allāh ﷻ the Most Beneficent, the Most Merciful and may peace and blessings be sent upon the beloved Prophet, Guide and Final Messenger, Muhammad ﷺ and upon his beloved family and Companions ﷺ.

A person will face many different challenges throughout their life. However, the beauty of Islām lies in the mere fact that it has all the answers to every possible situation. A Muslim may be struggling to cope, yet the holy Qur'ān and ahādīth are filled with antidotes to these struggles. As Muslims, we are encouraged to view our calamities as blessings. More so, it is an opportunity for us to turn to Allāh ﷻ with a sincere heart and strengthen our īmān (faith).

This entire universe was created by Al-Khāliq (The Creator). If we were to re-create a 'perfect world' how would we choose to create it? The answer is: exactly the same as it is now. Allāh ﷻ has created this world and it is perfect. Initially, it may be hard to understand that this world full of conflict, disease and murder is perfect. However, without tests, would our īmān remain strong? Would we still have the qualities of humbleness and gratefulness? There is always a reason behind these things. It is notable that all of these diseases and viruses are happening because of our own actions. We must accept this fact and then learn the best way to deal with this.

This short booklet outlines the ways in which we should deal with calamites. The solution is embedded with the majestic words of Allāh ﷻ and authentic ahādīth which serve as remedies to our problems. It is hoped that by reading this brief and concise booklet, the reader will be able to tackle calamities in the way our pious predecessors and mainly, the way our beloved Prophet Muhammad ﷺ did. In this way, the reader will be better equipped for the inevitable hardships that they will encounter in their lives.

Being Patient

We are living in times where the spread of disease is prevalent. For any individual, this may be challenging to deal with. However, Islām teaches us to take precautions and in fact, has clear instructions and guidelines for how to deal with any situation. This can be encompassed in the following verse:

وَلَنَبْلُوَنَّكُمْ بِشَيْءٍ مِّنَ الْخَوْفِ وَالْجُوعِ وَنَقْصٍ مِّنَ الْأَمْوَالِ وَالْأَنفُسِ وَالثَّمَرَاتِ ۗ وَبَشِّرِ الصَّابِرِينَ ۝

"And We will surely test you with something of fear and hunger and a loss of wealth and lives and fruits, but give glad tidings to the patient." (2:155)

If a student already knows what is going to be on the exam paper, they will prepare for it. Similarly, Allāh ﷻ has given us a clear message that He will test us all, so therefore, it is not something unexpected and we should prepare for it. Allāh ﷻ and His Messenger ﷺ clearly communicated all of these things to us.

Allāh ﷻ mentions the elements of fear and hunger. This is indicated by the words الْخَوْفِ وَالْجُوْعِ. This fear can indicate numerous things such as the loss of wealth, loss of family members, loss of productivity and many other types of losses. However, we must always remember the beautiful words وَبَشِّرِ الصّٰبِرِيْنَ **"But give glad tidings to the patient."** This is a subtle reminder that patience is rewarded. The next verse then encourages the following to be said when struck with a calamity:

إِنَّا لِلّٰهِ وَإِنَّا إِلَيْهِ رٰجِعُوْنَ

"Indeed, we belong to Allāh and indeed, to Him we will return." (2:156)

More commonly, this is said at the passing away of a Muslim brother or sister, but the reality is, we should form a habit of saying this at any calamity we face.

Turning to Allāh ﷻ

In every situation we must turn to Allāh ﷻ and remember the words mentioned above, which remind us that this world is only temporary. However, with the frequent spread of diseases, people shift into a state of panic and this is evident from those in the supermarkets fighting over toilet paper. It is these types of actions that are increasing. Instead, the shelves of Islamic bookshops should be empty to the extent where there are no copies of the holy Qur'ān remaining. People are supposed to be reading the holy Qur'ān day and night. They should be holding a tasbīh in their hands and doing abundant dhikr. That is how it should be, but instead, everybody is worried. Constantly worrying and frantically panicking.

وَلَنُذِيقَنَّهُم مِّنَ الْعَذَابِ الْأَدْنَىٰ دُونَ الْعَذَابِ الْأَكْبَرِ لَعَلَّهُمْ يَرْجِعُونَ ۞

"And We will surely let them taste the nearer punishment short of the greater punishment that perhaps they will repent." (32:21)

Allāh ﷻ is saying that we will taste the smaller difficulties before the bigger punishment. Why is this the case? To put it simply, as mentioned in the verse, it is so that you turn to Allāh ﷻ in repentance. Allāh ﷻ is so Merciful and gives us countless opportunities to turn to Him. He wants us to prepare ourselves before we go and meet Him, subhān-Allāh. A teacher does not write an exam paper for a student to fail. Likewise, Allāh ﷻ has not sent us to this world in order to punish us in the Hereafter. How Compassionate and Kind! Allāh ﷻ says:

مَّا يَفْعَلُ اللَّهُ بِعَذَابِكُمْ إِن شَكَرْتُمْ وَآمَنتُمْ ۚ وَكَانَ اللَّهُ شَاكِرًا عَلِيمًا ۞

"What would Allāh do with your punishment if you are grateful and you believe? And ever is Allāh Appreciative and Knowing." (4:147)

Subhān-Allāh, such a moving verse which brings tears to the eyes.

Allāh سبحانه وتعالى completely discards any form of punishment for those who do merely two things: be grateful for the blessings that Allāh سبحانه وتعالى has bestowed upon them and believe. In this world, you have to work tireless nights and long days to attain temporary success, but for an eternity of Paradise, we are merely required to do these two simple things, subhān-Allāh. Allāh سبحانه وتعالى says:

﴿وَإِن تَعُدُّوا نِعْمَةَ اللَّهِ لَا تُحْصُوهَا ۗ إِنَّ اللَّهَ لَغَفُورٌ رَّحِيمٌ﴾

"And if you should count the favours of Allāh, you could not enumerate them. Indeed, Allah is Forgiving and Merciful." (16:18)

It is impossible to count the blessings that Allāh سبحانه وتعالى has given us. Our hearts alone beat around 100,000 times a day without the need to think about it. This only takes place because of the mercy of Allāh سبحانه وتعالى. So, even during the times of a global pandemic, we must remember that Allāh سبحانه وتعالى is Al-Hakīm (The Wise). All things happen for a reason. During this time of isolation, when even the masājid are closed, we should turn towards Allāh سبحانه وتعالى. Allāh سبحانه وتعالى states in the holy Qur'ān:

وَمَآ أَصَٰبَكُم مِّن مُّصِيبَةٍ فَبِمَا كَسَبَتْ أَيْدِيكُمْ وَيَعْفُوا۟ عَن كَثِيرٍ ۝

"And whatever strikes you of disaster - it is for what your hands have earned but He pardons much." (42:30)

Accepting Responsibility

Difficult times that befall us are because of our own doings. It is common that we blame others for problems that arise, but instead, we should reflect upon ourselves and our own actions. You may have done over one hundred mistakes, one hundred sins, one hundred transgressions, but Allāh سُبْحَانَهُ وَتَعَالَىٰ does not hold you to account, because He has forgiven so many. Sometimes, Allāh سُبْحَانَهُ وَتَعَالَىٰ deliberately puts us in difficult situations in order that we turn back to Him. It can be said that this is a blessing in disguise, subhān-Allāh!

However, to respond positively to something such as a global pandemic does not come easily for a lot of us. As Allāh سُبْحَانَهُ وَتَعَالَىٰ says:

إِنَّ ٱلْإِنسَٰنَ خُلِقَ هَلُوعًا ۝

"Indeed, mankind was created anxious." (70:19)

How beautifully Allāh سُبْحَانَهُ وَتَعَالَىٰ summarises the nature of mankind:

إِذَا مَسَّهُ ٱلشَّرُّ جَزُوعًا ۝

"When evil touches him, he becomes impatient." (70:20)

This impatience is apparent from the masses of people panic buying and emptying the shelves of supermarkets, hoarding months worth of food. If this is the response to just a brink of difficulty, imagine what will happen when Dajjāl emerges.

The Biggest Trial

The emergence of Dajjāl will be a time where drought and famine will be widespread, which will result in global starvation and poverty. However, Dajjāl will have food and he will have the physical resources that everyone needs. He will also present Paradise in one hand and Hell in the other in order to mislead people. This will be the biggest test. This is the reason our holy Prophet ﷺ says:

وَإِنَّ مِنْ فِتْنَتِهِ أَنَّ مَعَهُ جَنَّةً وَنَارًا فَنَارُهُ جَنَّةٌ وَجَنَّتُهُ نَارٌ

"Part of his fitnah will be that he will have with him Paradise and Hell, but his Hell will be a Paradise and his Paradise a Hell." (Ibn Mājah)

It is important that we reflect and prepare for this time of great fitnah (temptation). When the Hour finally comes, people will become extremely selfish. Allāh ﷻ says in the Qur'ān:

يَوْمَ يَفِرُّ الْمَرْءُ مِنْ أَخِيهِ ۝

"On the day a man will flee from his brother." (80:34)

Subhān-Allāh, we will run away from our own family members. This is evident even now. During the coronavirus pandemic, many have become so worried to the extent they do not even want to leave the house. Everyone has this fear of contracting this virus, so they avoid even their own family members. This is exactly what will happen on the Day of Judgement. People will view their own relatives as diseased and dangerous, hence, they will flee. So it is integral that we prepare for this day.

Increase in Good Deeds

It is important that in the situations we face today, we turn to Allāh ﷻ. Secondly, we must accept that these calamities befall us because of our own doings. We must take responsibility for our actions and make plans to rectify ourselves. At the end of each day, reflect on your shortcomings and decide on how to improve yourself. Set goals and try to especially increase in good deeds. In the following hadīth, our holy Prophet ﷺ says:

بَادِرُوا بِالْأَعْمَالِ فِتَنًا كَقِطَعِ اللَّيْلِ الْمُظْلِمِ يُصْبِحُ الرَّجُلُ مُؤْمِنًا وَّيُمْسِي كَافِرًا أَوْ يُمْسِي مُؤْمِنًا وَيُصْبِحُ كَافِرًا يَّبِيعُ دِينَهُ بِعَرَضٍ مِّنَ الدُّنْيَا

"Be prompt in doing good deeds (before you are overtaken) by turbulence which would be like a part of the dark night. During (that stormy period), a man would be a Muslim in the morning and a disbeliever in the evening, or he would be a believer in the evening and a disbeliever in

the morning and he will sell his faith for worldly goods." (Muslim)

Encourage yourself to do as many good deeds as possible for the sake of Allāh ﷻ to avoid such fluctuation of īmān as demonstrated in this hadīth. We must ensure that we are performing our five daily prayers and we should even push ourselves to increase our salāh and nafl (optional) prayers.

However, sadly, instead of all this, we are seeing an increase in unnecessary shopping trips, the playing of games and other activities that waste this precious gift of time. In reality, we should be reciting more of the holy Qur'ān, doing istighfār and increasing our strength and connection with Allāh ﷻ.

Giving Sadaqah

In the hadīth it has been mentioned:

"Compete in giving sadaqah; indeed, the calamity does not surpass the sadaqah." (Tabarāni)

When you give sadaqah during a time of difficulty, the difficulty is eased. For this reason, it is beneficial to form a habit of giving sadaqah in the path of Allāh ﷻ. There are numerous opportunities for us to engage in this beautiful act as we now live in a technologically advanced world, alhamdulillāh. It takes just a couple of taps on your phone and subhān-Allāh, the money is sent within seconds. Whether you are donating to a masjid, a charity, or a poor individual in need, it should be done on a regular basis.

In the following hadith, there is a beautiful du'ā of the angels for a person who gives sadaqah:

مَا مِنْ يَوْمٍ يُصْبِحُ الْعِبَادُ فِيهِ إِلَّا مَلَكَانِ يَنْزِلَانِ فَيَقُولُ أَحَدُهُمَا اَللّٰهُمَّ أَعْطِ مُنْفِقًا خَلَفًا
وَيَقُولُ الْآخَرُ اَللّٰهُمَّ أَعْطِ مُمْسِكًا تَلَفًا

"There is never a day wherein servants (of Allāh ﷻ) get up at morning, but are not visited by two angels. One of them says, 'O Allāh ﷻ, give the one who spends (for the sake of Allāh ﷻ) a good reward,' and the other says, 'O Allāh ﷻ, bring destruction to the one who withholds." (Muslim)

Those who give in the path of Allāh ﷻ save themselves from facing the wrath of Allāh ﷻ and amazingly, it prevents the person from having a bad death. Forming a habit of giving, humbles a person and serves as a shield of protection. In this modern day and age, with fitnah everywhere, it is important that we take steps to safeguard ourselves and giving sadaqah is an excellent step towards this.

Du'ā is the Weapon of a Believer

Du'ā is indeed a very powerful weapon that each and every Muslim has been gifted with. It requires little but sincere effort and yields abundant good. In the holy Qur'ān Allāh ﷻ says:

﴿وَقَالَ رَبُّكُمُ ادْعُونِيٓ أَسْتَجِبْ لَكُمْ﴾

"Call upon Me, I will respond to you." (40:60)

We should always turn to Allāh ﷻ regardless of the situation we are in. Even when we are faced with news that may be difficult to bare, we should be grateful to Allāh ﷻ. Every individual person has their own tests, but in order to pass each test, we must all do the same, which is to turn towards Allāh ﷻ and make sincere du'ā.

Preventative Matters

In a pandemic as vast as the coronavirus, we may fear that we will contract the virus and therefore, lock ourselves in our homes for many months. Although this may be the initial reaction, we should look at the du'ās that our holy Prophet ﷺ has provided for us. Our beloved Prophet ﷺ has equipped us with du'ās for every single situation, subhān-Allāh!

In the following hadīth, our beloved Prophet ﷺ says:

مَا مِنْ عَبْدٍ يَّقُوْلُ فِيْ صَبَاحِ كُلِّ يَوْمٍ وَّمَسَاءِ كُلِّ لَيْلَةٍ بِسْمِ اللّٰهِ الَّذِيْ لَا يَضُرُّ مَعَ اسْمِهٖ شَيْءٌ فِي الْأَرْضِ وَلَا فِي السَّمَاءِ وَهُوَ السَّمِيْعُ الْعَلِيْمُ ثَلَاثَ مَرَّاتٍ فَيَضُرَّهٗ شَيْءٌ

"There is no person who says in the morning and evening of every day, 'In the name of Allāh, with Whose name nothing on earth nor in heavens harms and He is the All-Seeing, All-Knowing,' three times and is then harmed by anything." (Ibn Mājah)

A person who reads this du'ā three times in the morning and three times in the evening will be safeguarded from all calamities, disasters, ailments and all sicknesses.

Also, when we hear about illness anywhere, the holy Prophet ﷺ says in the following hadīth:

"Whoever sees an afflicted person and says:

اَلْحَمْدُ لِلّٰهِ الَّذِيْ عَافَانِيْ مِمَّا ابْتَلَاكَ بِهٖ، وَفَضَّلَنِيْ عَلٰى كَثِيْرٍ مِّمَّنْ خَلَقَ تَفْضِيْلًا

He (or she) will never by afflicted by it (this particular affliction)." (Tirmidhī)

Du'ā of Sayyidunā Anas ﵁

Another excellent du'ā to read is the du'ā of Sayyidunā Anas ﵁:

بِسْمِ اللّٰهِ عَلٰى نَفْسِيْ وَدِيْنِيْ، بِسْمِ اللّٰهِ عَلٰى اَهْلِيْ وَمَالِيْ وَوَلَدِيْ، بِسْمِ اللّٰهِ عَلٰى مَا اَعْطَانِيَ

اللهُ. اَللهُ رَبِّيْ لَآ أُشْرِكُ بِهٖ شَيْئًا . اَللهُ اَكْبَرُ اَللهُ اَكْبَرُ اَللهُ اَكْبَرُ وَاَعَزُّ وَاَجَلُّ وَاَعْظَمُ مِمَّا اَخَافُ
وَاَحْذَرُ عَزَّ جَارُكَ وَجَلَّ ثَنَاؤُكَ وَلَآ اِلٰهَ غَيْرُكَ . اَللّٰهُمَّ اِنِّيْ اَعُوْذُ بِكَ مِنْ شَرِّ نَفْسِيْ وَمِنْ شَرِّ
كُلِّ شَيْطٰنٍ مَّرِيْدٍ وَّمِنْ شَرِّ كُلِّ جَبَّارٍ عَنِيْدٍ . فَاِنْ تَوَلَّوْا فَقُلْ حَسْبِيَ اللهُ لَآ اِلٰهَ اِلَّا هُوَ عَلَيْهِ
تَوَكَّلْتُ وَهُوَ رَبُّ الْعَرْشِ الْعَظِيْمِ . اِنَّ وَلِيِّيَ اللهُ الَّذِيْ نَزَّلَ الْكِتٰبَ وَهُوَ يَتَوَلَّى الصّٰلِحِيْنَ

(I seek blessings) in the name of Allāh ﷻ upon myself and my religion. (I seek blessings) in the name of Allāh ﷻ upon my family, wealth and children. (I seek blessings) in the name of Allāh ﷻ upon all that which Allāh ﷻ has given me. Allāh ﷻ is my Lord. I do not ascribe anything to Him. Allāh ﷻ is the Greatest, Allāh ﷻ is the Greatest, Allāh ﷻ is the Greatest and Mightier and Majestic and Greater than all that I fear and all that I am wary of. Your protection is mighty and Your praise is great, and there is none to be served besides You. O Allāh ﷻ, indeed I seek protection in You from the evil of myself and from the evil of every accursed Shaytān and from the evil of every rebellious oppressor. ***Thus, if they (the rejecters) turn away, then say "Allāh is sufficient for me. There is no deity but Him." In Him alone do I place my trust and He is the Lord of the Mighty Throne. Indeed, my Guardian is Allāh Who revealed the book (the holy Qur'ān) and protects the pious.***

This is such an amazing du'ā which was taught by the holy Prophet ﷺ to Sayyidunā Anas ؓ. The story behind this du'ā is so remarkable, subhān-Allāh. A very well-known tyrant leader, Hajjāj ibn Yūsuf wanted to harm Sayyidunā Anas ؓ. Many times he would come prepared with his people and attempt to harm Sayyidunā Anas however, on every occasion he failed and Sayyidunā Anas remained untouched.

The surprising matter of this was that Hajjāj ibn Yūsuf was well known for his success in defeating and killing people. However, he could not lay a finger on Sayyidunā Anas. People became curious and began to question why he had failed to kill him. He had responded that every time he wanted to do something to Sayyidunā Anas, he saw two lions on either side of him, which would leap out in front and prevent him from striking Sayyidunā Anas, subhān-Allāh!

When Sayyidunā Anas was asked about his protection, he told the people that he had read this du'ā. It is such a beautiful du'ā that may be relatively long but is very effective in protecting one from harm. If a person reads this once in the morning and once in the evening, he will be safeguarded from a variety of calamities, disasters and ultimately, any harm whatsoever.

A Miraculous Incident
The Attempted Assassination

In 2019, a group of people attempted to assassinate Muftī Taqi Uthmānī Sāhīb (hafizahullāh). They surrounded him on their motorbikes from all angles and began to shower bullets towards him and his family members. During this time of distress, Muftī Sāhīb had asked his family members if they had read du'ā-e-Anas and they all replied that they had. He then said to his family, "Do not worry about it. In that case, nothing can harm us." Allāhu Akbar!

Not a single bullet touched any of the members who had read duā-e-Anas. This is a great example of yaqīn (certainty in faith). Nowadays, this level of yaqīn is rare to find. As Muslims in this modern day, we lose sight of the power of Allāh ﷻ and become hypnotised by the illusions of the dunyā, when in reality, we should always remember that Allāh ﷻ is Al-Hāfidh - The Protector. As long as we have yaqīn in Allāh ﷻ, we will be protected.

Cleanliness

In times of a pandemic, people wear face masks and gloves, but when you ask if they have read any duās for protection, the answer is no. There is so much certainty that these physical items will prevent any viruses entering our body, but more importantly, we also need spiritual protection which can only come from Allāh ﷻ.

However, this does not mean we should just roam around without any protection during a global pandemic. Instead, we should adhere to advice sought from health professionals. Advice that Islām has already obligated to follow.

Look at how beautiful our Islām is! Subhān-Allāh, it is a requirement to wash our hands five times a day for wudhū and a sunnah to wash our hands after waking up. This is mentioned in the following hadīth:

إِذَا اسْتَيْقَظَ أَحَدُكُمْ فَلْيُفْرِغْ عَلَى يَدِهِ ثَلَاثَ مَرَّاتٍ قَبْلَ أَنْ يُدْخِلَ يَدَهُ فِي إِنَائِهِ فَإِنَّهُ لَا يَدْرِي فِيمَ بَاتَتْ يَدُهُ

"When anyone amongst you wakes up from sleep, he should wash his hands three times before putting it in the utensil, for he does not know where his hand was during the night." (Muslim)

It is also a requirement that we must wash ourselves properly after using the bathroom. There is such a huge emphasis on tahārah (cleanliness) that our holy Prophet ﷺ says:

اَلطُّهُورُ شَطْرُ الْإِيمَانِ

"Cleanliness is half of faith." (Muslim)

The status of cleanliness in Islām is such that without it, half of our dīn remains incomplete. Allāh ﷻ also says in the Qur'ān:

وَثِيَابَكَ فَطَهِّرْ ﴿٤﴾ وَالرُّجْزَ فَاهْجُرْ ﴿٥﴾

"And purify your clothing. And avoid uncleanliness." (74: 4-5)

Allāh ﷻ is clearly instructing us to purify ourselves and avoid remaining in an unclean state. Being physically pure also cleanses our īmān and protects us from many illnesses and sicknesses. It is not a coincidence that the guidelines set by doctors and consultants today are in sync with what the holy Prophet ﷺ had said and done over 1400 years ago, subhān-Allāh! Therefore, it is key that we follow and adhere to these guidelines as much as we can. Not only do we receive protection from these illnesses, but just doing these basic acts, such as washing your hands will earn us immense rewards (in-shā-Allāh).

Coach Incident in Bangladesh

I was on my way travelling back from Cox Bazar in Bangladesh. Me and my colleagues had halted at a location as we had seen a coach collide and fall into a ditch. There were many passengers on the coach who were screaming and crying out in pain. Many had broken backs, legs, arms and other severe injuries. We stopped our van immediately and attempted to help them as best as we could. We called a few passers-by to help and then proceeded to wait for the arrival of an ambulance and the police.

When the authorities came to the scene, we knew they were in safe hands and prepared to leave. However, some people refused to let us go. I remember a particular individual who called out to me and said, "Shaykh, don't go! Please pray to your Allāh that He takes away this problem and heals the injuries! Pray to your Allāh that He grants us recovery!" I was startled and confused by this response.

Then, one of my colleagues told me that these passengers who were on the coach were not even Muslims. They were Hindus, subhān-Allāh! Tears began strolling down my cheeks and I said to myself, "You are our Allāh ﷻ; You are our Creator!" These people have just come out of their idol-worshipping temples, yet they do not have yaqīn in their gods, but they have yaqīn in our Allāh ﷻ. They have yaqīn that our Allāh ﷻ is going to heal them of their injuries and that our Allāh ﷻ is going to solve their problems, subhān-Allāh!

This was such a beautiful and inspirational incident. It is a reminder that we are indeed very fortunate to be Muslims. At that particular moment, the following Qur'anic verse came to my mind:

﴿ٱلۡحَمۡدُ لِلَّهِ ٱلَّذِي هَدَىٰنَا لِهَٰذَا وَمَا كُنَّا لِنَهۡتَدِيَ لَوۡلَآ أَنۡ هَدَىٰنَا ٱللَّهُ﴾

"Praise be to Allāh, Who has guided us to this and we would never have been guided if Allāh had not guided us." (7:43)

The Value of Īmān

Sometimes, we may get caught up in the craze of the dunyā and start to value our īmān less and less. When it comes down to the value of īmān, we must ponder upon those pious predecessors such as Sayyidunā Bilāl ؓ, Sayyidunā Salmān Fārsi ؓ and Sayyidunā Suhaib

Rūmi ﷺ. They endured unimaginable pain and atrocities, yet their īmān was always so strong.

This is also the case with reverts. They also value their īmān greatly. We hear about their stories and their journey back to Islām and the persecution they suffered at the hands of their own family members or local community and it makes us realise that we have got it very easy. This is the very reason why we do not value our īmān as much. However, this should not be an option for us; we must value our īmān.

Allāh ﷻ has provided an antidote for every situation and calamity that we will encounter in this dunyā. We do not need to panic. The mark scheme for this dunyā is already mentioned in the holy Qur'ān which means we do not need to stress. Allāh ﷻ says,

قُل لَّن يُصِيبَنَا إِلَّا مَا كَتَبَ اللَّهُ لَنَا هُوَ مَوْلَانَا ۚ وَعَلَى اللَّهِ فَلْيَتَوَكَّلِ الْمُؤْمِنُونَ ۝

"Never will we be struck except by what Allāh decreed for us; He is our Protector and upon Allāh should the believers trust." (9:51)

Whatever was written for us will happen by the will of Allāh ﷻ.

Sayyidunā Abū Ubaidah ibnul Jarrāh and the Plague

Sayyidunā Umar was in the land of Shām, today known as Syria. He was leading the Muslim forces to gain control over Shām. As he was travelling with his entourage towards Shām, they were given the news about a plague. He was unsure whether to continue the expedition or to leave and head back. After consulting the senior Companions and considering the situation, he decided to take himself and the rest of the Companions back in the morning.

When Sayyidunā Abū Ubaidah ibnul Jarrāh met Sayyidunā Umar, he asked him, "Are you fleeing from the decree of Allāh?" Sayyidunā Umar replied:

نَعَمْ نَفِرُّ مِنْ قَدَرِ اللهِ إِلَى قَدَرِ اللهِ

"Yes, we are running from the divine decree of Allāh to the divine decree of Allāh." (Bukhārī, Muslim)

Subhān-Allāh! The underlying point from this story is that whatever is going to happen will happen with the taqdīr (decree) of Allāh. We need to ensure that we do our part; there should be no panic-buying and living in fear but instead we should remain calm and live in contentment.

We must also carry out the points that have been mentioned. So firstly, we must turn towards Allāh ﷻ. Secondly, we must increase in the good deeds that we do. Thirdly, we must increase in the act of sadaqah. Finally, we must take preventative measures by reciting the du'ās that have been narrated in the authentic ahādīth, as well as paying attention to hygiene.

Attending the Masjid During a Pandemic

If one falls ill, the general ruling that the jurists have mentioned is that if the illness results in the emission of foul odours from the individuals body, he should not attend the masjid. In this instance, he should pray salāh at home. Although this may be difficult for the person to accept, they will still receive the same reward as praying salāh in congregation in the masjid, which is 27 times more reward, subhān-Allāh! This is what we sometimes lose sight of. Allāh ﷻ has truly made it easy for every individual. Even if a sick person cannot carry out usual acts of worship which they used to carry out when they were healthy, they will still get rewarded for the acts of worship in full. Allāh ﷻ has opened the door for us to earn rewards. So even if we are in a state where we have contracted a disease, we should be grateful to Allāh ﷻ as this is what was written for us.

Abiding by the Laws

If the government lays out an order for social distancing to take place and as a result, masājid are closed, we must abide by this. So long as these rules do not go against Islamic principles, we must adhere to them. Many of us ignore this and say, "We are Muslims; we must attend the masjid no matter what!" This is the incorrect stance to take. Instead we are ordered to follow the guidelines of the country we live in. Subhān-Allāh, the sheer beauty of Islām is unquestionable.

This also applies to speed limits! Many of us can get too comfortable with the gas pedal whilst on the motorway which means we exceed the speed limit. However, if we exceed the limits set by the law, we will not only incur a hefty fine and some penalty points, but more seriously, we will be sinful in the eyes of the Sharī'ah. It is key that we always keep these points in our mind, as it will dictate the decisions we make and the way we live our lives. Islām is not just a set of rules and guidelines but a way of life for us all. We must try our best to follow and emulate the way of our beloved Prophet ﷺ.

May Allāh ﷻ increase us in our Īmān and forgive our shortcomings. Āmīn!

A MUSLIM'S GUIDE TO CORONAVIRUS

IN LIGHT OF THE BLESSED AHĀDĪTH OF RASŪLULLĀH ﷺ

ĀPĀ SAHLA BEGUM

Foreword

All praise is due to Allāh ﷻ, the Sole Originator of the universe. May Allāh's ﷻ infinite peace and blessings be upon the Messenger of Allāh ﷺ, our beloved leader and guide, Muhammad ﷺ.

During these uncertain times, the belief and īmān of the Muslims around the globe is being tested. It is at times like this, we are to hold firm to the guidance of our beloved Messenger ﷺ more than ever.

This short compilation of ahādīth along with a brief commentary has been authored by my dear friend and sister in Islām, Āpa Sahla, a graduate from JKN Institute, Bradford. She is currently teaching hadīth at Zaytūn Institute in Leeds. May Allāh ﷻ accept her efforts and reward her with goodness in both this life and the Ākhirah.

Please keep us and the rest of the Muslim Ummah in your sincere du'ās. May Allāh ﷻ lift this calamity from us and grant all those who have passed away due to this plague the highest rank in the Hereafter and accept them as shahīd!

آمیـــــــن یا ربّ العالمین

Khādimatul 'Ilm
May 2020

Introduction

When this coronavirus crisis erupted, it brought with it many effects in the everyday lives of all of us. One such effect has been the plethora of information going around on social media. Although much has been beneficial, there have been many controversial posts. Furthermore, it has been quite amazing that the majority of people are pretty well versed when it comes to topics such as 'coronavirus symptoms', or 'lockdown rules in the UK' due to the usage of social media but sadly, not many Muslims can boast of such in depth knowledge on what Allāh سبحانه وتعالى and His Messenger ﷺ say regarding such trials of life.

Through studying and teaching the ahādīth regularly, I have noticed that each and every hadīth has a wisdom and a relevance to our current situation in a beautiful manner. From some, new perspectives can be derived, whilst for others, the original meanings come to life in a way which may not have been fully appreciated before. It is for this reason that this treatise has been compiled. I pray Allāh سبحانه وتعالى enlightens our hearts with the blessed words of His beloved Messenger ﷺ and may He alleviate from us the difficulties of this calamity. Āmīn!

Āpa Sahla Begum
Graduate of JKN Institute
Teacher at Zaytūn Institute
April 2020

تُحفَةُ المُؤمِنِ المَوتُ

"Death is a gift for the believer."

Baihaqī in Shu'abul Īmān

Death is a Gift for the Believer

The world is brought to a standstill. Everywhere we turn we see social restrictions, closures, lockdowns and panic. There is a great fear within us all. What if my loved one catches it? Will they suffer its torture in solitude? Or will I lose them? What if I catch it? What will happen to me? Will I die a lonely death all alone without any family? How could this be? Is there a cure or will it wipe us all out? The fears are intense. The questions are endless.

But for a true believer, our beloved Prophet ﷺ has said, "The gift of the believer is death." Why? Because a believer is hopeful of meeting his Most Compassionate, Loving, Nurturing Lord and he is not attached to the lowly life of this world. He sees the ***real*** life as the life of the Hereafter and his heart yearns towards it.

So let us ask ourselves, where do we fall in the above types of people? Are we the fearful people filled with panic? Or are we at peace, knowing that death will meet us anyway, coronavirus or no coronavirus? And if the answer is not the latter, then it's not too late. Let us turn back to our Lord and let go of our lowly attachments to this fleeting life. Let us turn our attention to the inevitable eternal life of the Hereafter to which we are all heading whether we like it or not. Let us reconnect with our Master and yearn for Him and then inshā-Allāh, if Allāh ﷻ wills, for us death will be our gift.

اَلطُّهُورُ شَطْرُ الْإِيمَانِ

“Purity is half of faith.”

Sahīh Muslim

Purity is Half of Faith

"Wash your hands! Wash your hands! Wash your hands!"

These are the repetitive words we are all hearing in this coronavirus crisis and this was the first point of advice by our government and health professionals. It is such a simple instruction, yet it is so apparently weighty in light of the current situation. It begs the question; were people not already washing their hands? The sad reality is, for many, the answer is no, or at least, not enough.

Whereas, our beautiful religion has taught us to wash our hands all the time. Over 14 hundred years ago, before the age of modern technology and healthcare, our beloved Prophet ﷺ instructed us that we must wash our hands at the time of waking, before and after eating, when using the toilet and 5 times a day for wudhū. If we were to do the maths, this is in fact, a lot of hand washing!!

And it does not stop there. Our beautiful religion further teaches us to bathe regularly, to brush our teeth many times a day, to clean inside our nose, to be conscious of our mouth and body odour, to keep our yards tidy which in turn signifies the importance of keeping our homes tidy and the list can go on.

Once, a Companion of the beloved Prophet ﷺ, Salmān al-Fārsi رضي الله عنه was mocked regarding the minute and sometimes graphic (in as respectable manner as possible) details of purity mentioned by our noble Prophet ﷺ. He responded in confidence that there is no shame in this and that we are proud and grateful to be taught such everyday essentials!

It is no wonder then that our beloved Prophet ﷺ has said, "Purity is half of faith." How well he has described the great lengths our religion underwent in order to preserve our cleanliness and how sad it is to see that we Muslims have forgotten our own religion.

Now we are all rushing to the shops to buy out the hand washes. Now we are all careful to cover our mouths and noses during sneezing and coughing. Now we are all super sensitive with regards to our cleanliness. But did it require a deadly disease and a global crisis to hit us in order for us to act upon the wise and intelligent teachings of our beloved Prophet ﷺ?

Let us rekindle our zeal to understand our comprehensive religion and in turn, let us act upon its beautiful and practical teachings in the hope of being rewarded in the Hereafter and protected in this life. Let us keep washing our hands and maintain general hygiene, not just because of the coronavirus, but out of love and trust for our beloved master, Prophet Muhammad's ﷺ exemplary teachings. And in the process, may it be a means of our protection from this testing disease and all other diseases and more importantly, may it be a means of our salvation. Āmīn!

كَفَى بِالْمَرْءِ كَذِبًا أَنْ يُحَدِّثَ بِكُلِّ مَا سَمِعَ

"It is enough for a person to prove himself a liar when he goes on narrating whatever he hears."

Sahīh Muslim in his Muqaddamah

Narrating Everything You Hear

Social media is like a double-edged sword; either it can be used for good or it can be used for bad. During this coronavirus epidemic, social media has acted no differently. Many are the encouraging, thought-provoking reminders, be they about the teachings of Islām or general positive reports. However, sadly, we are also seeing a plethora of negative feeds.

Whether it be false lockdown threats, theories of the Chinese being punished, suspicions of helicopters depositing chemicals on us or people going round spreading their germs on car door handles, the conspiracy theories have been coming thick and fast.

Furthermore, the information overload we are all exposed to, due to the lengthened periods of time we spend on our phones, creates a sense of anxiety and fear which is unprecedented amongst the masses. If we were to ask ourselves, how would this news have come to us around 10 years ago when social media was not so prominent, we would come to the conclusion that save some news reports at certain times of the day and possibly some newspaper articles, our exposure to such news was minimal in comparison to today's time.

Everyone from the girl next door to the leaders of the world are posting feeds of all kinds. Every time we pick up our phones we are being bombarded with coronavirus updates on a local, national and even a global level. All we see is coronavirus, coronavirus,

coronavirus!

Before anything is even happening people are panicking beyond reason. Stockpiling is occurring everywhere well in advance of any form of lockdown taking place totally disregarding any logical understanding of social distancing. People are obsessively suspicious and vigilant about the contact they are having with others even their own family members. Fear is rife in everyone.

But where is the limit to all this information overload? Where do we draw the line of beneficial and unbeneficial? The answer can be found in the beautiful teachings of our beloved Prophet ﷺ. He has advised us, "It is sufficient for a person to be a liar that he relates everything he hears." This is a stark warning for us when it comes to relating news. The key point here is that we must be conscientious as to how much we relate, even if it is true. Yes, even if it is true, we could be classed as a liar in the sight of Allāh ﷻ and His Messenger ﷺ, if we are reporting too much. This is because chances are, if you are posting anything and everything, sooner or later, you will narrate something false.

So next time we are about to send out a post or forward a text, let us remember our beloved Prophet's ﷺ warning and ask ourselves, is it true? Can we verify the information? And on top of this, will it truly be of benefit to us? Or will it contribute to the information overload and the excessive fear mongering taking place amongst us? Will it only increase us in anxiety or will it bring us closer to our objective in pleasing Allāh ﷻ and finding peace at a time when we need it the most?

اَلدِّيْنُ النَّصِيْحَةُ

"The religion (of Islām) is sincerity."

Sahīh Muslim

The Religion is Sincerity

This is one of the shortest of the ahādīth but despite consisting of only two words, it carries a heavy meaning which requires further explanation. Thus, it is not surprising that when the holy Prophet ﷺ said this, a noble Companion asked him who this sincerity should be directed towards. The beloved Prophet ﷺ explained, "For Allāh ﷻ, for His Book, for His Messenger ﷺ, for the leaders of the Muslims and ***for the general public."*** It is the last part of this hadīth which I wish to discuss.

As Muslims, we should be sincere in our advice and well-wishing of one another. This means just as we would like for somebody to advise us well or wish the best for us in our time of need, we too should also wish the same for others . The holy Prophet ﷺ said, "None of you truly believes until he loves for his brother what he loves for himself." (Bukhārī)

It is a real shame that during this never witnessed before global crisis, we Muslims are doing the very opposite. We have people stocking up goods at home, in order to save themselves and their families from any discomfort whilst others are left without even their basic necessities due to the empty shelves. It is like a domino effect; once the first people go out and stockpile, others feel the need to do so in fear of finding the shelves empty and thus, the fear spreads and tawakkul in Allāh ﷻ being our Provider withers. And to make matters worse, the retail companies are boosting their prices to take advantage of the weakness of the people. How sad a state of affairs! Where is the sincerity in this?

And it doesn't stop here. All over the country, we are being advised to practice social distancing in order to prevent the spread of the disease. "STAY AT HOME," we are told, not only to protect ourselves but more so to protect the vulnerable amongst us who are likely to be hit the worst. It is a communal effort which must be done in congregation just as the Jumu'ah Salāh is performed in congregation. Yet, we still see some brothers and sisters so confident that they will be "fine" going on with their lives as normal and totally disregarding any forms of precaution. They show little care or consideration for the way their behaviour is effecting everyone around them and putting people at risk, potentially leading to a life or death outcome. This is not sincerity and these are not the teachings of our religion.

We should have love, concern and consideration for one another at all times; especially more so in times of crisis like this. As Muslims, we should be the first to follow the guidance and unite for the sake of sincerity towards others.

We see around us many people taking on the community spirit and helping others, however they can, out of sincerity, be it through supporting in the burial process, supporting the elderly, shopping for others or even simply a kind word. The kindness and sincerity has been heart-warming. Let us Muslims not fall behind in these ways and let us be the pioneers of sincerity during this testing time, representing the teachings of our beautiful religion Islām. Let us embrace the brief yet concise, wise words of our beloved Prophet ﷺ by truly demonstrating our sincerity. Then, and only then, will we be truly upon the religion.

اِعْقِلْهَا وَتَوَكَّلْ

"Tie it (the camel) and have trust (in Allāh)."

Jāmi' At-Tirmidhī

Trusting in Allāh ﷻ and Tying the Camel

This is one of the most referred to of the ahādīth during this pandemic leading to many questions; how much precautions should we be taking around our families? Should we visit the sick? Do we attend the masjid? Should we still be going to work? These are the types of questions we are suddenly presented with and many a debate has arisen.

There are always two extreme ways of reacting in every situation.

You have some who are utilising every worldly means possible to stay protected. They will stay at home no matter what the outside needs may be to the extent that they hoard goods which are much needed by everyone in the community. Some will avoid everyone at all costs, often offending people. Others, deep clean everything and even impose their extreme practices on others around them. Heavily influenced by those who have no belief in Allāh ﷻ, they fail to realise that if Allāh ﷻ wills, they will catch the disease even if they were in strong fortified towers. They disregard Allāh's ﷻ power and have little or no trust in Him despite Him being the Controller of everything, including the very virus they are striving to save themselves from.

Then, you have the other extreme of people who will simply say, "Allāh ﷻ will protect me," yet they do not do anything to save themselves. They do not educate themselves on the issue nor practice any precautionary hygiene measures and then they walk around amongst the people as normal with no concern of spreading the disease. They disregard the responsibility they have towards not only their own lives but also for the lives of others.

We as Muslims must ask ourselves where do we lie on the scale? Are we leaning too much towards the worldly precautions and not putting enough trust in Allāh ﷻ? Or are we being neglectful of precautions and ignoring the reality of the world around us?

Each of us will be somewhere on the scale but the best place to be is on the middle ground. Allāh ﷻ has called us a 'moderate nation' so we should be taking our worldly precautions and leave our trust with Allāh ﷻ; we must tie our camels and have tawakkul. Only then will we be reassured that our way of dealing with this great trial is according to what Allāh ﷻ and His Messenger ﷺ would like. Only then will we feel at peace with ourselves.

إِنَّمَا الأَعْمَالُ بِالنِّيَّاتِ

"Actions are according to intentions."

Sahīh al-Bukhārī & Muslim

Actions Are According to Intentions

Very rarely is any hadīth compilation void of this precious hadīth. This is its power and in this coronavirus crisis, it could not be any more appropriate and relevant to mention it.

Most of us are cooped up at home, out of routine and adapting to many everchanging circumstances around us. Whether it be mums having to adjust to having the whole family at home all day and cooking twice as much, dads missing their outside space and worrying about their financial responsibility or kids just having to cope with everything with their little minds, we are all more or less in the same boat.

Some of us may see it as a burdensome affair; "We don't get to see our friends," "I am getting sick of seeing the same four walls!" or "How many hours have I been on my phone again?" are just some of the questions we may find we are asking ourselves.

Yet, if we were to look a little deeply into the situation and see the positive side of things, we would notice many a blessing in our situation and our intentions are the key.

So when a busier than ever mum under lockdown next makes the ever growing number of daily meals for her family, let her shift her intention that she is feeding her family to give them strength to be good servants of Allāh ﷻ; in this way a seemingly worldly action like cooking will become an act of worship. When a father is helping the kids with their school work, let them have the intention of acting upon the Qur'anic āyah "Iqra!" so that they can utilise the rare opportunity to educate their children and make it a means of reward. When the sibilings are helping their parents with extra household chores, let them have the intention of being dutiful to their parents and the reward will be immense.

It is all about the intention; with the correct intention, all good actions can become a means of reward. So today, whilst we are all adjusting to the fast paced changes in all of our lives due to this crisis, let us take a moment to adjust our intentions alongside the adaptations and inshā-Allāh, with Allāh's ﷻ help, rather than being a burden, this lockdown could become a huge means of reward for us all.

اَللّٰهُمَّ إِنِّيْ أَعُوْذُ بِكَ مِنَ الْهَمِّ وَالْحَزَنِ، وَالْعَجْزِ وَالْكَسَلِ، وَالْجُبْنِ وَالْبُخْلِ، وَضَلَعِ الدَّيْنِ، وَغَلَبَةِ الرِّجَالِ

"O Allāh! I seek refuge with You from worry and grief, from incapacity and laziness, from cowardice and miserliness, from being heavily in debt and from being overpowered by (other) men."

Sahīh al-Bukhārī

A Comprehensive Du'ā

Of the many supplications which the holy Prophet ﷺ taught us, we can find much to console us in these testing times. But in this particular supplication there appears to be a special relevance. Despite there being many mini supplications within this du'ā, the way that each and every single individual request is incredibly relevant to our current situation is just amazing! It almost feels as though Allāh ﷻ knew that we would be in this exact situation now so He taught this du'ā to the holy Prophet ﷺ over 1400 years ago! Its words come to life in a real way for us when we witness and experience how much each of the things which the holy Prophet ﷺ taught us to ask Allāh ﷻ for refuge from are the exact things which very many of us are facing on a daily basis:

1. ANXIETY: Who amongst us can say that this calamity has not made us feel anxious? Very little or maybe none of us could say it has not. People are anxious about their lives, their health, their wealth and their families which are arguably the most important aspects of everyone's lives. The anxiety created by this crisis has been immense. Thus, we need to ask Allāh ﷻ for safety from it.

2. DEPRESSION: The daily news of the number of people dying is very depressing for all and what makes it worse is knowing how these people died alone. It has been a very sobering time for all of mankind and hence, important for us to seek refuge in Allāh ﷻ from

demobilising depression.

3. LACK OF ABILITY: Many a time, anxiety and depression can cause demotivation. Our spirits can become weak and we may find ourselves not having the motivation to get up and do our usual day to day ibādah and activities. Thus, it's important to ask Allāh ﷻ to protect us from this loss of morale and grant us the ability to continue on with our lives and thrive no matter the circumstances.

4. LAZINESS: Being in lockdown means we have less external distractions in our lives and more time on our hands. If this time is not used in a productive way, we could become lazy and useless. Some may spend all day on their phones, scrolling through random, unnecessary information, others may watch TV all day, others may play computer games; the pastimes are many but usually, in such times, a sense of laziness develops so we must ask Allāh ﷻ to save us from this.

5. LACK OF COURAGE: Fear is a huge feeling amongst the masses. Many are afraid of catching the disease and having themselves and their families suffer. This fear can become so strong that people forget that everything happens by the will of Allāh ﷻ and courage to reach out and help others becomes deficient. This then creates a selfishness that can become consuming. Therefore, it is also important that we are brave during this trial and that we try our level best to not only function as normal but utilise the reminder and opportunity to do good. This requires courage and hence, we

seek refuge in Allāh ﷻ from lack of courage.

6. DEBT: Financial problems are a big worry for many during these times. Many people are losing their jobs or having to take time off work leaving them struggling to make ends meet. It has been a very real aspect of this crisis and we may feel the need to borrow money just to keep things going but left worried about how or when to pay this back. Thus, an important prayer during these times is to seek refuge in Allāh ﷻ from debts.

7. OVERPOWERING OF MEN: Often, difficult times lead to bad behaviour within people. Lockdown restrictions lead to frustration and anger. People become irritated and overwhelmed and lash out. It is not surprising that cases of domestic violence have risen during the lockdown. Furthermore, when people are in financial restraint, this can lead to problems amongst people such as a lenders demanding their money back. In these ways, people can become overpowered by others, thus, we ask for Allāh ﷻ for protection from being overpowered by men.

May Allāh ﷻ keep us protected from all of the above things during these testing times. May He help us and mankind and relieve us of this deadly virus and its effects and make it a means of mercy, guidance and blessings for us. Āmīn!

I pray that Allāh ﷻ grants us all the true understanding of the ahādīth of His beloved Messenger ﷺ and gives us the ability to act upon them in this life in order to gain salvation in the next!

آمیـــــــــن یا ربّ العالمین

Quranic Wonders

The science of Tafsīr in itself is very vast, hence the compilation of these specific verses provides the reader with a simple and brief commentary. It is aimed to equip the reader with a small glimpse of the profound beauty of the Holy Qur'ān so that they can gain the passion to study further in depth. It is hoped that this will become a means of encouragement to increase the zeal and enthusiasm to recite and inculcate the teachings of the Holy Qur'ān into our daily lives. **UK RRP:£5:00**

Protection in the Grave
Sūrah Al-Mulk encapsulates the purpose of our creation - that we were created to live a life of obedience to our Lord and Creator. This can only be made to manifest through our good deeds which we perform solely for the sake of Allāh ﷻ, in order to seek His pleasure. The Holy Prophet ﷺ told his Ummah to recite this Sūrah every night and learn this Sūrah by heart. The importance of this Sūrah is stressed due to the fact that the Holy Prophet ﷺ never slept until he had finished reciting this Sūrah. **UK RRP:£4:00**

Protection from Black Magic
These last ten Sūrahs are not only distinct in their meanings and message which will be discussed in this book, but also the fact that every Muslim should have these Sūrahs committed to memory as a minimum requirement in seeking refuge in Allāh ﷻ from all harm and evil, and every imperfection as well as seeking solace and peace in understanding His might and attributes. **UK RRP:£5:00**

Nurturing Children in Islam
Bringing up children has never been an easy duty. The challenges do not get easier as they get older either. Our emotions and other priorities sometimes hinder in nurturing our children, and as such, we fail to assist our children in reaching their potential by continually stumbling over our own perception of what we consider as ideal children. Our duty to our children is not without accountability. Our neglect and lack of interest in our children will be held to task. **UK RRP:£5:00**

Ready for Judgement Day?
For those that doubt the Day of Resurrection, Allāh ﷻ is reaffirming that there is no scope for uncertainty; this day is indisputable and will surely occur. The day when the truth will be laid out bare and everything will be exposed, there will be no place to flee or escape to. Regretting that day will be of no avail; excuses will fail to safeguard or shelter a person from breaking free and escaping judgement. **UK RRP:£4:00**

Flee Towards Allāh ﷻ
Sūrah Al-Ma'ārij begins by addressing the disbelievers who used to mock the Holy Prophet ﷺ about the Day of Judgement. In this Surah, Allāh ﷻ severely reproaches those who deny it assuming that there is only one life; the life of this world. The Sūrah manifests its horrors and catastrophic scenes that the entire creation shall witness on that very day. Mankind will then realise that on this horrific day, they will be judged by their own actions. **UK RRP:£4:00**

Lanterns of Knowledge
Once the commentary of Kitābul 'Ilm in Bukhāri was completed, we realised that this chapter is an entire topic in itself due to its fascinating and insightful perspective on knowledge. When compiling this commentary, there were many beautiful reminders as well as points of guidance for everyone's personal life as well as their lifelong quest for knowledge. Therefore, the commentary of this chapter alone would be beneficial for all seekers of knowledge and the idea of publishing it as a separate book came to mind. **UK RRP:£10:00**

TIME IS RUNNING OUT
As the title suggests, as each day passes, we come closer to our death. Life is too short to be treated as an amusement and for the fulfillment of one's lust. The Day of Judgement is inevitable where we all must one day stand in front of the Lord of the Worlds to give an account of our deeds. These six Sūrahs explain the horrors and terrifying moments of Judgement Day and the inevitable standing before the Lord. We must therefore prepare for the Hereafter by realizing our purpose in life; to worship Allāh ﷻ Alone and reduce our worldly expectations. **UK RRP:£4:00**

Best of Stories

Sūrah Yūsuf is more than just a story of one of our beloved Prophets there is much wisdom and lessons to be learnt and understood. All th knowledge comes from our honourable Shaykh, inspiration and Ustādl Shaykh Mufti Saiful Islām Sāhib. May Allāh shower Mufti Sāhib wit mercy and accept the day in, day out effort he carries out in the work c Dīn. **UK RRP:£4:00**

Call of Nuh

For 950 years, Sayyidunā Nūh persevered night and day in continuous succession in preaching the message; unwavering and relentless in his mission. Not once did he feel that his calling was in vain. He stood firm and resolute in continuing with the mission that he was sent with, in proclaiming the message of the oneness of Allāh ; year after year, decade upon decade, century after century, but this failed to convince the people of the truth. **UK RRP:£4:00**

A Glimpse of Paradise

Time is the true wealth we have at our disposal though it cannot be amassed. The only way we can utilise it to our advantage is when we do righteous deeds and actions; for this will act in our favour in the Ākhirah (Hereafter). These moments will be preserved in exchange for moments of greater happiness and bliss in the next life. Therefore, we need to perform righteous deeds and actions in the short duration of time we have at our disposal in this temporary worldly life.

UK RRP:£4:00

Six Qualities of a Believer

Respected readers, do you want to be successful in this life and the Hereafter? The fact that you have prompted yourself to pick up this book and read, is an indication that the answer is *yes*. Or perhaps, you were not aware of the contents and purpose of this book and hence, eternal success wasn't the first thing on your mind. Nonetheless, it is easy to turn your attention towards this objective right now. **UK RRP:£2:00**

Living Islām in Modern Times

This book is a compilation of various articles written by Shaykh Dr. Rafāqat Rashīd Sāhib in the popular Al-Mu'min Magazine. Considering the great benefit these articles will bring to the Ummah, Mufti Saiful Islām Sāhib decided to edit and transform them into a book format, making the content easily accessible for readers.

UK RRP:£4:00

A CLEAR VICTORY

This book "A Clear Victory" is an enlightening commentary of Sūrah Al-Fath. It is cited in Sahīh Al-Bukhāri regarding the virtue of this Sūrah that Sayyidunā Umar Ibn Al-Khattāb ﷺ reported that the Messenger of Allāh ﷺ said: "This night a Sūrah was sent down to me that is more beloved to me than all what the sun shines over," then he read, "*We have indeed accorded a triumph to you, a manifest triumph, indeed*". **UK RRP:£5:00**